Enjoy Playing Guitar

Christmas Crackers

**14 easy arrangements
with flexible accompaniments**

Debbie Cracknell

MUSIC DEPARTMENT

OXFORD
UNIVERSITY PRESS

OXFORD
UNIVERSITY PRESS

Great Clarendon Street, Oxford OX2 6DP,
United Kingdom

Oxford University Press is a department of the University of Oxford.
It furthers the University's objective of excellence in research, scholarship,
and education by publishing worldwide. Oxford is a registered trade mark of
Oxford University Press in the UK and in certain other countries

First published 2015

Impression: 1

ISBN 978–0–19–340716–9

Music and text origination by Katie Johnston
Printed in Great Britain on acid-free paper by
Halstan & Co. Ltd., Amersham, Bucks.

Christmas Crackers

How to use this book

A versatile resource, this collection includes the melodies and words to your favourite Christmas pieces plus accompaniment options for all occasions. Developing guitarists can play the carol or song as a solo, as part of a duet with the bass part or strummed chords, or as part of a quartet or larger ensemble. The collection can also be used to accompany singers, in which case players should consider using capos to take the tune to a comfortable pitch. Bracketed dynamics show those to be followed on repeats.

The MELODY and ACCOMPANIMENT Parts 2 and 3 can be played by elementary level guitarists (approximately Grades 1–3). ACCOMPANIMENT Part 1 is easier still and can be played by near beginners; the note-knowledge required for this part is shown at the start of each score.

For guitarists more used to acoustic styles, there are chord symbols above the ACCOMPANIMENT scores and a corresponding table of chord boxes on page 32. And if that isn't enough, try adding percussion—sleigh bells in 'Jingle, Bells' (four-bar intro and from bar 21) and 'Sleigh Ride' (bars 17–32 and coda), or maracas in 'The Virgin Mary had a baby boy'. Many of the pieces can be extended through creating introductions based on the first or last few bars.

Here's wishing you a fun-filled Christmas play-along!

Frosty the snowman

Words by Walter E. 'Jack' Rollins
Music by Steve Nelson

MELODY

Moderato

Frost - y   the   snow - man   was   a   jol - ly   hap - py   soul,   With a
Frost - y   the   snow - man   is   a   fai - ry   tale   they   say,   He was

corn - cob   pipe   and a   but - ton   nose   And two   eyes   made   out   of   coal.
made   of   snow   but the   chil - dren   know   How he

came   to   life   one   day.   There   must have been some   ma - gic   in that   old   silk   hat they

found,   For   when they placed   it   on   his   head   He be - gan   to   dance   a -

- round.   Oh,   Frost - y   the   snow-man   was a - live   as   he   could   be,   And the

chil - dren   say   he could   laugh   and   play   Just the   same   as   you   and   me.

Thum-pe - ty   thump, thump,   thum-pe - ty   thump, thump,   look   at   Frost - y   go.

Thum-pe - ty   thump, thump,   thum-pe - ty   thump, thump,   o - ver the   hills   of   snow.

ACCOMPANIMENT

• Part 1 uses G, A, B, C, C♯, and D on strings 2 and 3.

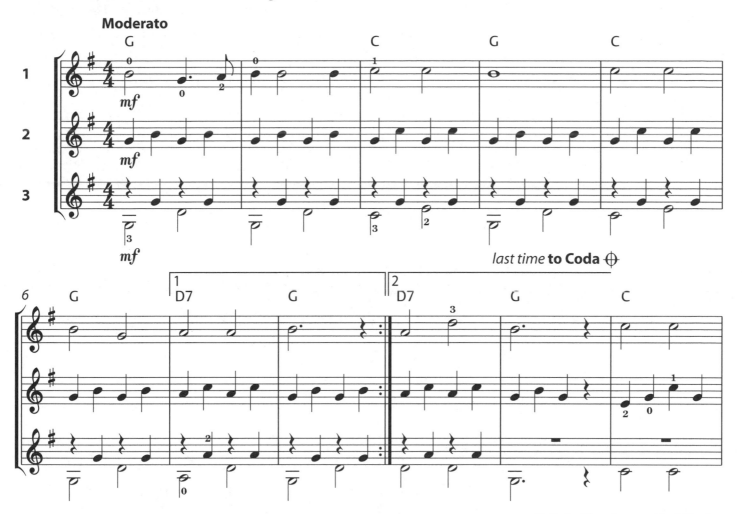

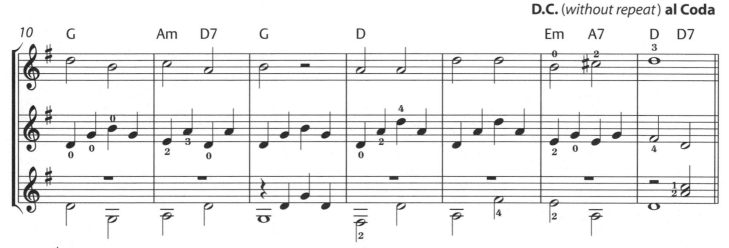

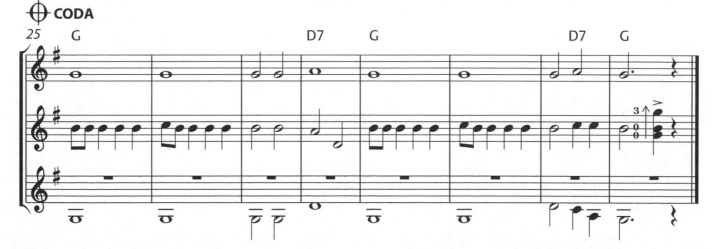

Away in a manger

Words 19th-cent. American
Music by W. J. Kirkpatrick

MELODY

Tranquillo

mp (repeat tasto)

A - way in a___ man - ger, no___ crib for a bed, The___
cat - tle are___ low - ing, the___ ba - by a - wakes, But___

5

lit - tle Lord Je - sus laid___ down his sweet head; The
lit - tle Lord Je - sus no___ cry - ing he makes. I

9

stars in the___ bright sky looked down where he lay, The___
love thee, Lord___ Je - sus! Look___ down from the sky, And___

13

lit - tle Lord Je - sus a - sleep in the hay. The nigh.
stay by my side un - til___ morn - ing is

tasto = play over the fingerboard

ACCOMPANIMENT

• Part 1 uses B, C, D, and E on strings 1 and 2.

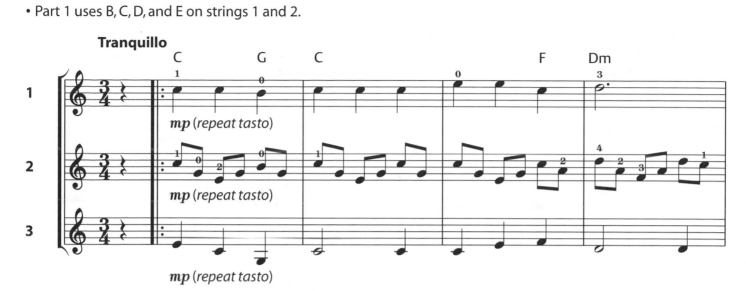

tasto = play over the fingerboard

Deck the hall

Welsh trad.

MELODY

Briskly, in 2

Deck the hall with boughs of hol - ly, Fa la la la la, fa la la la;
Fast a - way the old year pass - es, Fa la la la la, fa la la la;

'Tis the sea - son to be jol - ly, Fa la la la la, fa la la la.
Hail the new, ye lads and las - ses, Fa la la la la, fa la la la.

Fill the mead cup, drain the bar - rel, Fa la la la la la la la la;
Laugh - ing, quaff - ing, all to - geth - er, Fa la la la la la la la la;

Troll the an - cient Christ - mas ca - rol, Fa la la la la, fa la la la.
Heed - less of the wind and wea - ther, Fa la la la la, fa la la la.

ACCOMPANIMENT

- Part 1 uses D, E, and F on string 4.
- Part 2 is a descant—only play this part on the repeat.

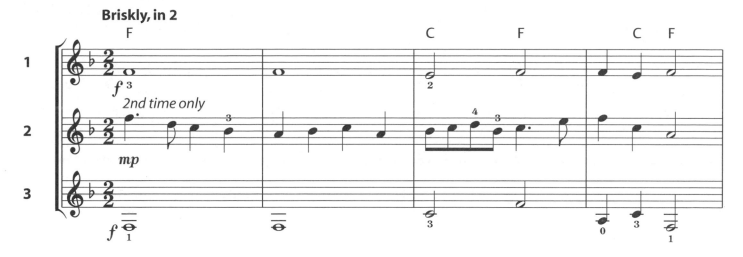

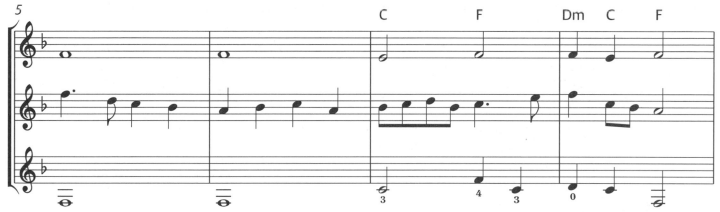

Let it snow!

Words by Sammy Cahn
Music by Jule Styne

MELODY

ACCOMPANIMENT

• Part 1 uses G, A, B, C, C#, and D on strings 2 and 3.

Once in royal David's city

Words by C. F. Alexander
Music by H. J. Gauntlett

MELODY

Once in roy - al Da - vid's___ ci - ty Stood a

low - ly cat - tle___ shed, Where a mo - ther laid___ her___

ba - by In a man - ger for___ his___ bed: Ma - ry

was that mo - ther mild, Je - sus Christ her lit - tle___ child.

ACCOMPANIMENT

• Part 1 uses G, B, C, and E on strings 1, 2, and 3.

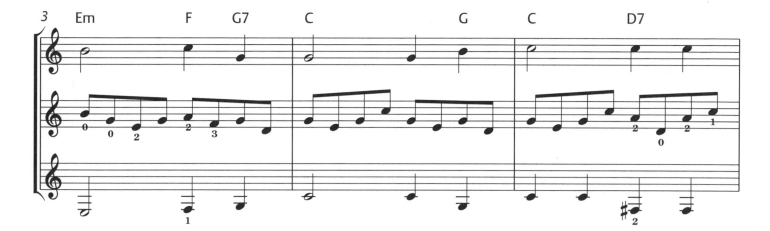

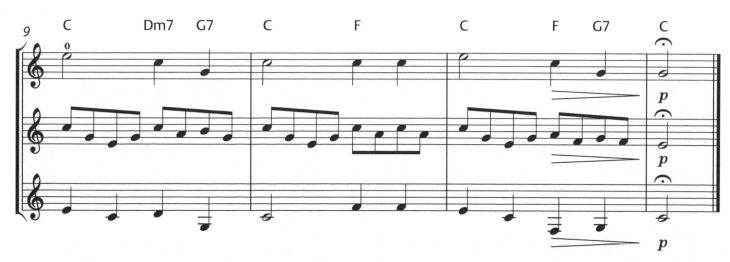

In dulci jubilo

(In sweet rejoicing)

Old German carol

MELODY

ACCOMPANIMENT

- Part 1 uses G, A, and B on strings 2 and 3 and octave harmonics on strings 3 and 4.
- When playing the repeat, the harmonic section could be played again to form a link passage. Otherwise, repeat from the upbeat to bar 5.

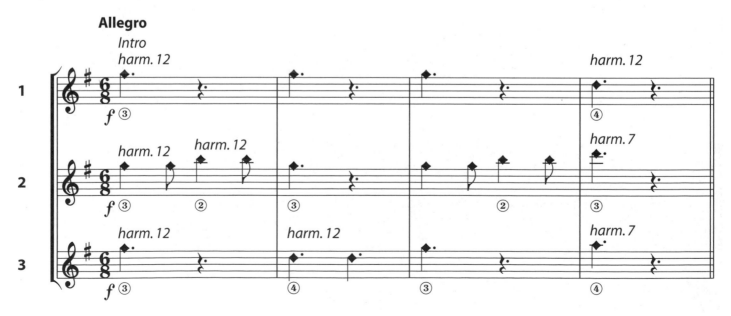

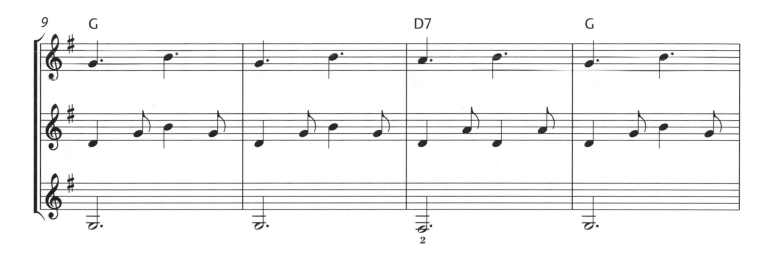

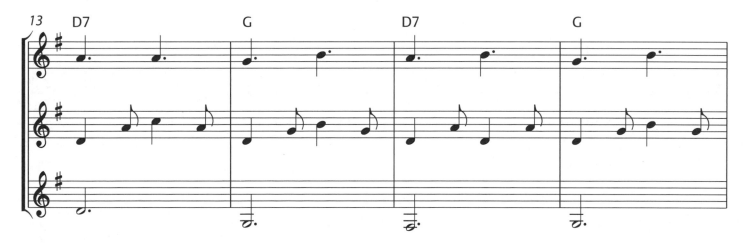

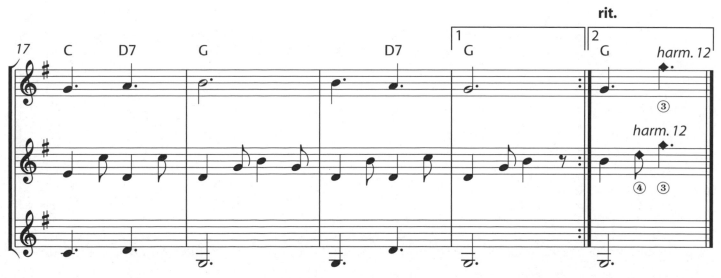

The Virgin Mary had a baby boy

MELODY

West Indian trad.

The Vir-gin Ma-ry had a ba-by boy,— the Vir-gin Ma-ry had a ba-by boy,— the Vir-gin Ma-ry had a ba-by boy, and they say that his name was Je-sus. He come from the glo-ry,— he come from the glo-ri-ous king-dom. He come from the glo-ry,— he come from the glo-ri-ous king-dom. Oh yes, be-liev-er! Oh yes, be-liev-er! He come from the glo-ry,— he come from the glo-ri-ous king-dom.

ACCOMPANIMENT

• Part 1 uses G, B, C, D, E, F, and high G on strings 1, 2, and 3.

*Tap on the body of the guitar, above the strings with the thumb and then below the strings with the fingers.

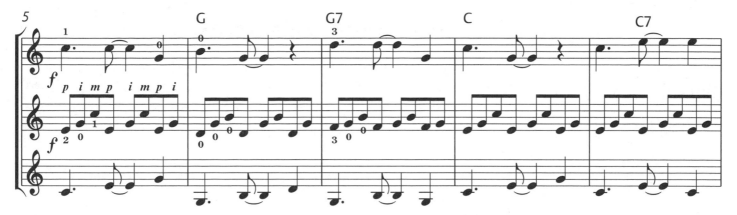

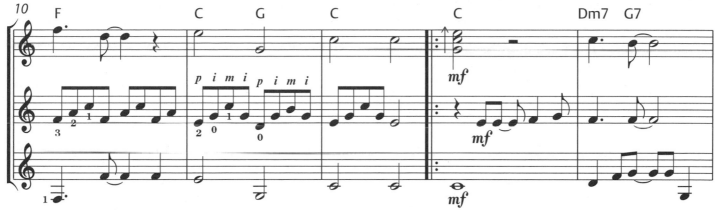

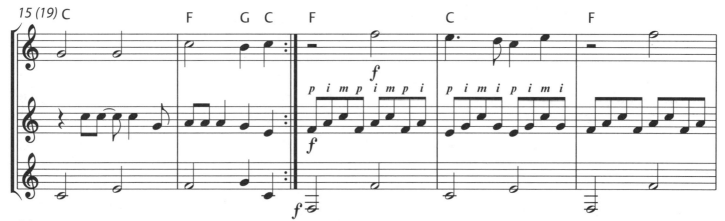

We wish you a merry Christmas

MELODY

English trad.

ACCOMPANIMENT

• Part 1 uses B, C, D, E, and F on strings 1 and 2.

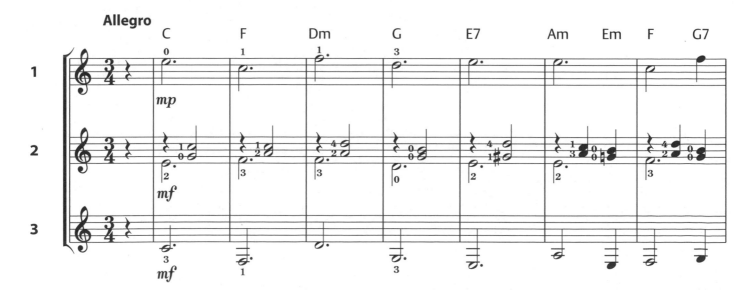

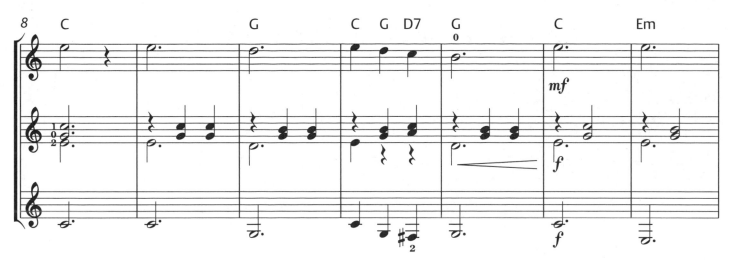

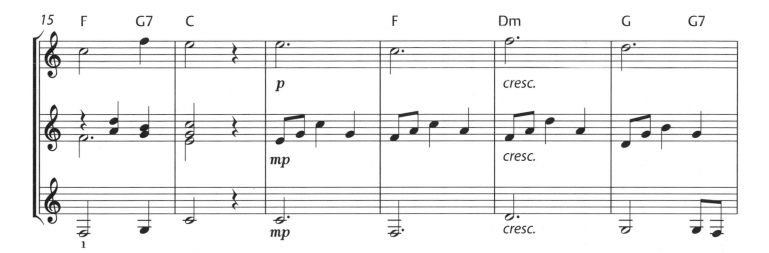

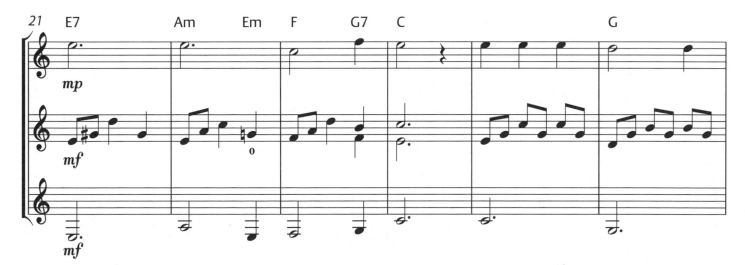

Rockin' around the Christmas tree

Words and music by
Johnny Marks

MELODY

ACCOMPANIMENT

• Part 1 uses C♯, D, D♯, and E on strings 1 and 2.

Hark! the herald-angels sing

Words by Charles Wesley and others
Music by Felix Mendelssohn

MELODY

Hark! the he - rald - an - gels sing___ Glo - ry to the new - born King;

Peace on earth and mer - cy mild,___ God and sin - ners re - con - ciled:

Joy - ful all ye na - tions rise,___ Join the tri - umph of the skies,___

With th'an - gel - ic host pro - claim, Christ is___ born in Beth - le - hem.

Hark! the he - rald - an - gels sing Glo - ry___ to the new - born King.

ACCOMPANIMENT

• Part 1 uses G, A, B, C, and D on strings 2 and 3.

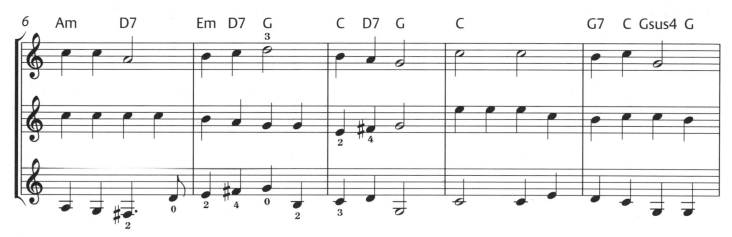

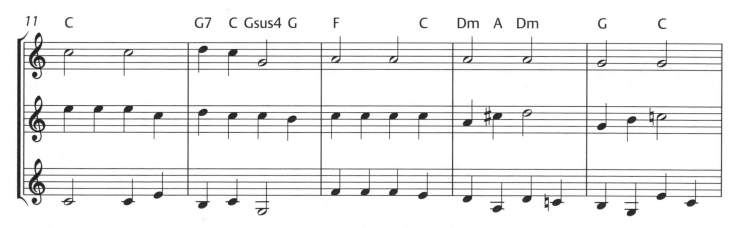

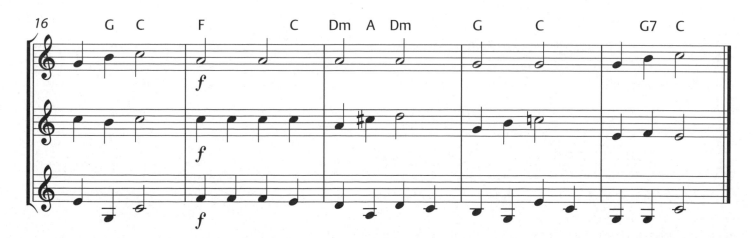

Jingle, Bells

Words and music by
J. Pierpont

MELODY

ACCOMPANIMENT

• Part 1 uses C, D, E, and F on strings 1 and 2.

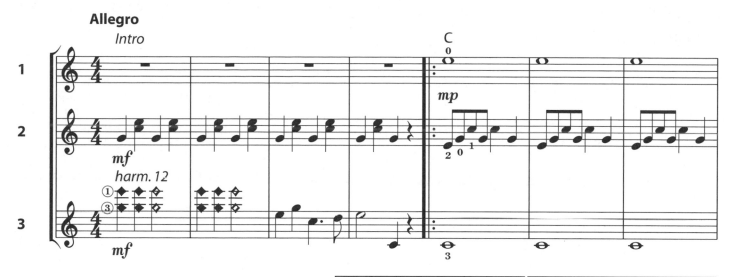

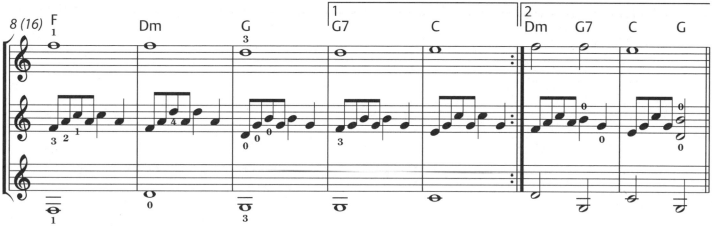

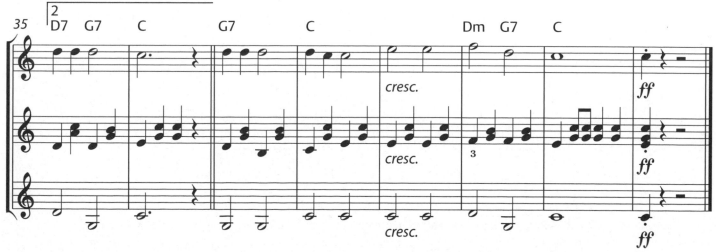

Santa Claus is Comin' to Town

Words by Haven Gillespie
Music by J. Fred Coots

ACCOMPANIMENT

• Part 1 uses G, A, B, and C on strings 2 and 3.

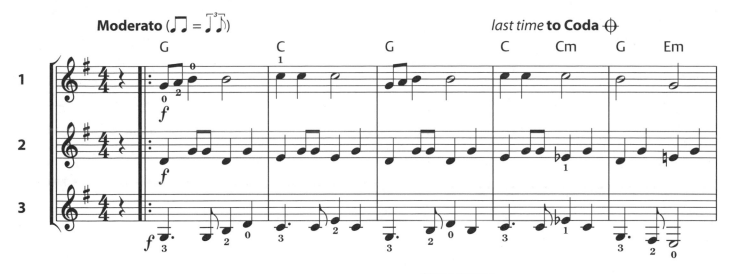

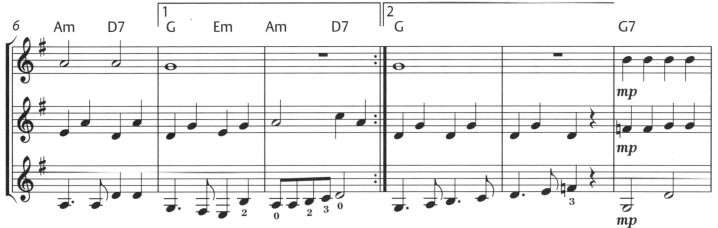

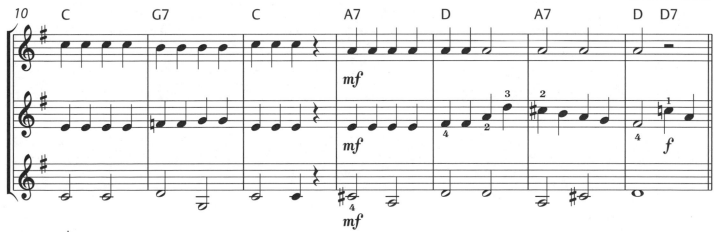

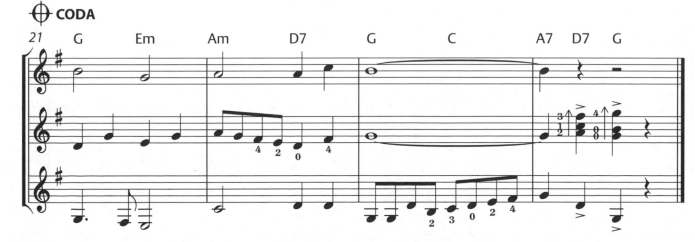

O little town of Bethlehem

Words by Phillips Brooks
Music English trad.

MELODY

O lit - tle town of Beth - le - hem, How still we__ see thee lie!
A - bove thy deep and dream-less__ sleep The si - lent__ stars go by.

Yet__ in thy dark__ streets shin - eth The ev - er - last - ing

light; The hopes and fears of all__ the years Are met in__ thee to - night.

ACCOMPANIMENT

• Part 1 uses A, B, C#, and D on strings 2 and 3.

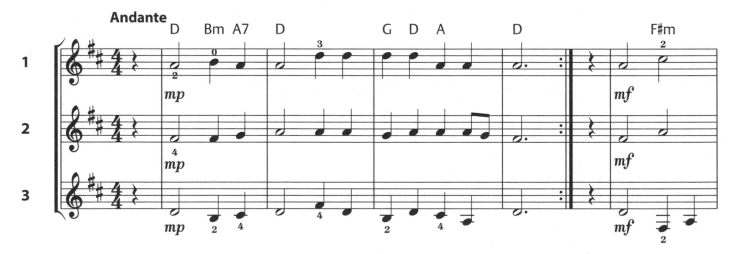

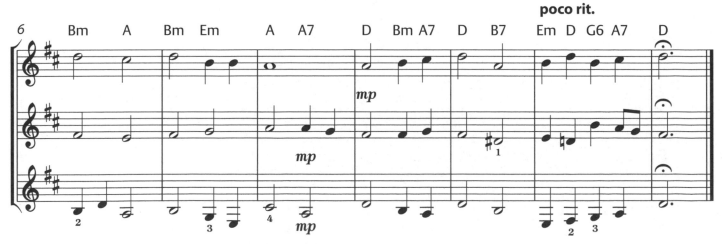

Sleigh Ride

W. A. Mozart (1756–91)
(from *Three German Dances*, K.605)

MELODY

ACCOMPANIMENT

• Part 1 uses G, A, B, C, and D on strings 2 and 3.

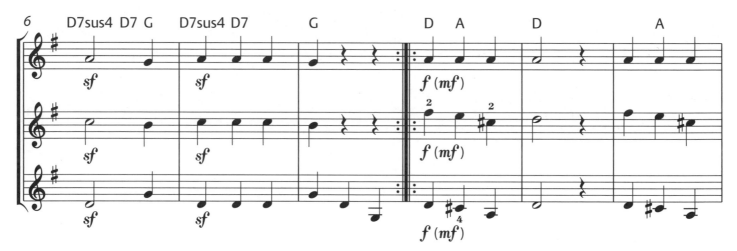

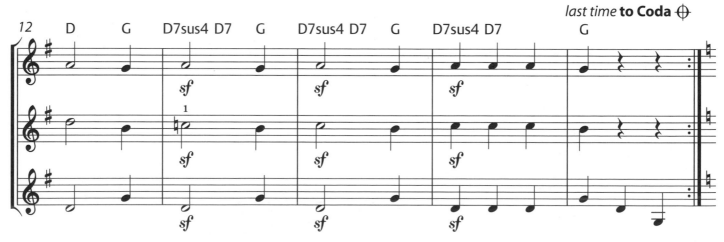

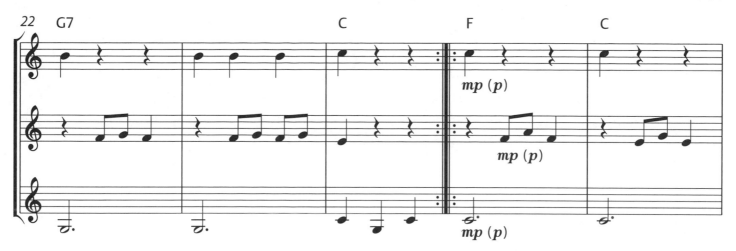

2nd time **D.C.** (*without repeat*) **al Coda**

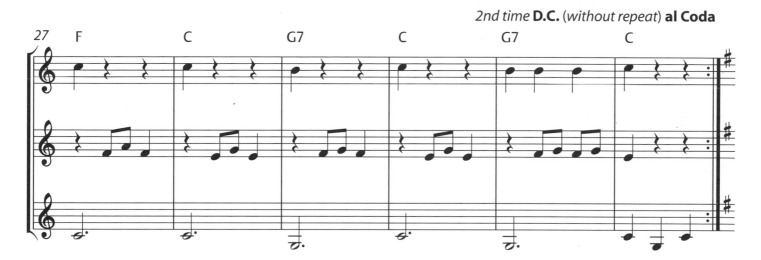

CHORDS

Strummed chords can be added to many of the pieces in this book, by reading the chord symbols above ACCOMPANIMENT Part 1. Here are the corresponding chord boxes:

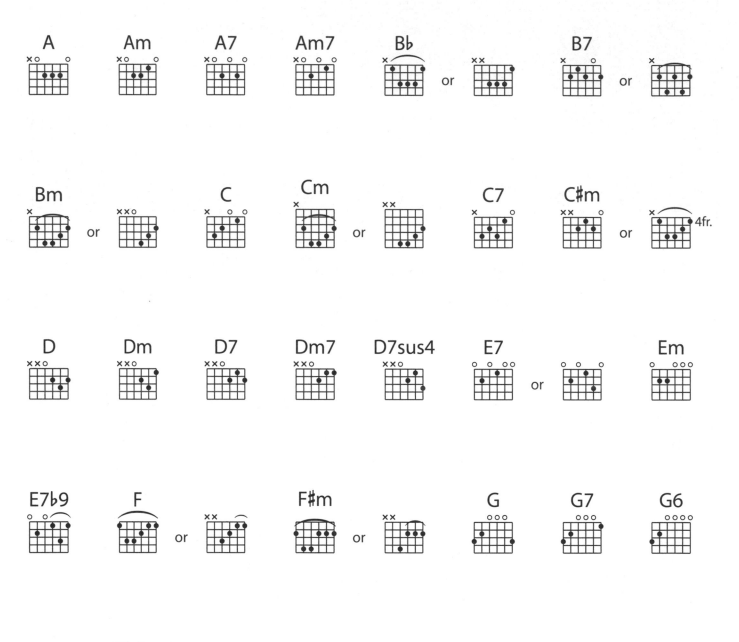